PAPER CUTTING
FOR CELEBRATIONS

100+ Chinese Designs for Festive Holidays and Special Occasions

Zhao Ziping

Better Link Press

On page 1
Double birds on plum blossoms.

Top on facing page
The owl represents wisdom.

Bottom on facing page
A pair of love birds perched on a branch stare lovingly at each other as flowers bloom all around them, just like a couple deeply in love.

Copyright © 2014 Shanghai Press and Publishing Development Company

All rights reserved. Unauthorized reproduction, in any manner, is prohibited.

This book is edited and designed by the Editorial Committee of *Cultural China* series

Text and Works by Zhao Ziping
Translation by Kayan Wong
Photographs by Liu Shenghui
Cover Design by Wang Wei
Interior Design by Yuan Yinchang, Li Jing, Hu Bin (Yuan Yinchang Design Studio)

Editor: Wu Yuezhou
Editorial Director: Zhang Yicong

Senior Consultants: Sun Yong, Wu Ying, Yang Xinci
Managing Director and Publisher: Wang Youbu

ISBN: 978-1-60220-149-1

Address any comments about *Paper Cutting for Celebrations: 100+ Chinese Designs for Festive Holidays and Special Occasions* to:

Better Link Press
99 Park Ave
New York, NY 10016
USA

or

Shanghai Press and Publishing Development Company
F 7 Donghu Road, Shanghai, China (200031)
Email: comments_betterlinkpress@hotmail.com

Printed in China by Shanghai Donnelley Printing Co., Ltd.

1 3 5 7 9 10 8 6 4 2

CONTENTS

Paper cutting, as the name implies, is the process of using a pair of scissors to cut a thin, flat sheet of paper into different shapes. Before the invention of paper, the art of paper cutting did not exist. However, through various carving techniques, the art of cutting and engraving on different thin materials such as gold, leather, silk, and even tree bark had been popular for ages. These techniques set a strong foundation for the development of paper cutting.

A Brief History

The history of Chinese paper cutting began with the appearance of paper. With the invention of paper during the Han Dynasty (206 B.C.–220 A.D.) came the development and popularization of paper cutting. In 1967, in the Astana tombs near the Xinjiang Turpan Basin Gaochang Ruins, archeologists found floral paper cutting artifacts dating from the Southern and Northern Dynasties (420–589). These ritual paper cuttings were made from hemp paper, and are the earliest physical evidence of Chinese paper cutting, dating back over 1,500 years.

By the Tang Dynasty (618–907), paper cutting had gone through a major period of development. The artwork housed at the British Museum show that paper cuttings from the Tang Dynasty already possessed rich picture composition as well as a variety of uses and purposes. For example, folklore used paper cuttings to conjure up spirits. People also cut thick paperboards into flower shapes, and used them to dye floral patterns onto fabric. On the Start of Spring in the 24 Solar Terms, people also cut paper into shapes

On facing page
Add paper cut designs to an ordinary, single-colored gift bag or wine tote to immediately bring it to life. Plum blossoms, bamboo, and the paradise flycatcher bird are all beautiful patterns with auspicious meaning in Chinese culture.

"Pairs of Monkeys" paper cutting fragments (reproduction).

Chinese shadow puppets (image from Quanjing).

of banners, butterflies, and money, and would wear them on their heads or adorn them on windowpanes to welcome the arrival of spring.

As paper production matured by the Song Dynasty (960–1279), the varieties of paper available also increased. This helped establish the popularity of paper cutting. In wedding ceremonies, red paper cutting art pieces adorned everything from bridal dowry boxes to gifts from guests. Wedding halls were also decorated with numerous floral cutouts on windows. The patterns and methods of paper cutting were also used on animal skins (cowhide, horse hide, sheepskin, etc.) to create shadow puppet figures. During a performance, artists stand behind white curtains and manipulate the opera characters. They

sing popular folk songs of the day, accompanied by percussion and string instruments, for an experience of distinctly local flavors. Shadow puppetry is an ancient traditional folk art form of the Han Chinese. With the economic and cultural development of the day, professional paper cutting artists and patterns also proliferated.

Paper cutting artwork from the Yuan Dynasty (1206–1368) were intricate, full-concept pieces that reached the same status as calligraphy paintings by famous artists, and thus people began to collect paper cutting art.

By the Ming and Qing dynasties (1368–1911), paper cutting art craft matured and reached its peak. Use of paper cutting became increasingly broad.

Decorations on lanterns, designs on fans, and embroidery patterns were all derived from paper cuttings as a basis. They were also used to decorate around the home, such as on windows and as decals on cabinets and lights. Patterns also became more rich and abundant; there are birds and fish, flowers and plants, bridge and pavilion sceneries, etc. New designs are freely improvised to the artist's heart's content.

A phoenix-patterned paper cutting on a lamp.

After centuries of evolvement, modern paper cutting is even more innovative than traditional paper cuttings. Most traditional paper cutting patterns were passed down through generations. But modern patterns have a strong contemporary sense both in colors and in composition. Their uses have also broadened: product packaging, fashion design, book covers, stamps, even animation and film reflect the signs of paper cutting.

The art of paper cutting developed over the long course of history. Its unique popularity, practicality, and aesthetics give it a timeless vitality as that of an ivy—ancient yet evergreen and alive.

A red paper cutting on window grilles (image from Quanjing).

Artistic Characteristics

Since its birth, Chinese paper cutting had enriched people's daily lives and left its mark on many cultural activities. The extensive flourishing of paper cutting art demonstrates people's pursuit and longing for beauty. The artistic characteristics of Chinese paper cutting can be broadly grouped into the following four points.

Life-related. Since ancient times, the creators of paper cutting were ordinary folks. This activity was a pastime, a hobby. Therefore, the subject and content of paper cuttings were intertwined with the creators' life, and their ideals and aspirations of a better life. For example, when a woman gets married, her relatives and even the bride herself would cut out "grape vines and squirrels" as a wish for blessings of many children and much happiness.

Exaggerated. Exaggerated distortion is another distinctive characteristic of paper cutting art. In traditional paper cutting crafts, you may find a large peony on the body of a fat pig. Normally, in daily life, large peonies do not appear together with pigs. But in paper cutting, the emphasis is on the meaning of "wealth and richness" represented by both the peonies and the pig. Thus, traditional paper cutting emphasizes "sentiment" over "subject," as well as "meaning" over "reality."

Symbolic. After centuries of development, several major themes have evolved for paper cutting. Patterns include people and figures, animals, plants, flowers, Chinese characters, geometric shapes, etc. Creators use objects' inherent meanings as well as names and homophones to create symbols of good outcomes and messages of well wishes.

Colorful. Because the creativity behind paper cutting relies on a single sheet of paper, choice of color is a major factor. Color choice in Chinese paper cutting tends to be simple and elegant, with an eye towards harmony. Generally speaking, choice of color tends to be bright and deep. Sometimes, emphasis is placed on color contrast, such as red with yellow. When shapes and colors work together, a whole static picture can come alive with movement and rhythm.

All in all, these artistic characteristics of Chinese paper cutting reflect the cultural and historical heritage of China, based on the constant innovation towards aesthetic beauty.

A large peony on a fat pig symbolizes abundant wealth and riches.

Using Paper Cutting Crafts as Decorations in Daily Life

The pursuit of beauty has existed since ancient days. Paper cutting has long been used as decorative flourishes on gift-wrap. Modern assembly lines have created arts and crafts that all look the same, greatly reducing the value of each item. In contrast, a unique, personally created handicraft would warm the heart of the recipient. At the same time, modern production technology has vastly increased the available choices of paper, greatly broadening the possibilities of paper cutting. Below are some examples.

Furniture. Is your single-colored lampshade too monotonous? Do your brown cabinets look too dull? Or is the design on your door too old-fashioned? If so, choose your desired pattern, cut it out, and attach it to the place where you'd like to see a style change for an immediate improvement. Imagine the warm yellow light glowing through the beautiful shapes on the lampshade, projecting patterns around the room. It definitely warms the heart.

Home décor. Paper cutting can be placed on window grilles. This decorative technique is ancient, and it remains a great way to decorate a transparent window, especially during holidays and festivals. If windows and glass doors are too clear, put a beautiful paper cut design on the window to prevent guests from walking into the glass. You can also use thicker paper to cut out contemporary designs, and add tassels, sequins, and beads to create curtains, ornaments, wind chimes, door banners, and decorations for a living room.

Utensils. Tired of the same pattern on your detachable travel mug? Don't rush out to buy a new one just yet. Measure the mug, choose a paper you like, cut your desired pattern, and place on the mug for a new look. During festivals or weddings, use paper cuttings as snack liners, cup and utensil decorations for a unique oriental look.

Gift-wrap. Unique and innovative gift packaging can bring a box to life. Aside from ribbons, paper cutting is a great choice as well. Choose the pattern based on the gift recipient, the original design of gift-wrap, or the occasion.

Sticker. There are numerous notebooks, greeting cards, and envelopes at the store. To set them apart, use paper cuttings as stickers and paste onto covers to increase the decorative value, as well as add a little fun to them.

Bookmark. How can you forget a chic bookmark to keep track of your reading progress? At the store there are long rectangular bookmarks as well as magnetic bookmarks. Why not try a paper cutting bookmark? Choose a favorite color, pick a thicker stock of paper; you can even choose a pattern that matches the story or the theme of the book. This way, the bookmark can be integrated with the book as a single work of art.

Gift. Create an exquisite, complex paper cutting project. For example, cut out different patterns based on a theme, then group them together and paste them onto a single background to form a complete scene or picture. The finished product can be framed for your own home, or be given as a gift to a friend.

Chinese Paper Cutting

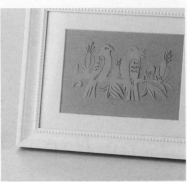

Gift Decoration

Artistic Inspiration

Creative
Idea

Chinese

Characters

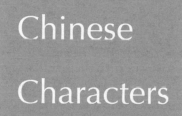

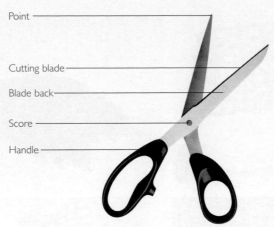

Point

Cutting blade

Blade back

Score

Handle

Parts of a pair of scissors (image from Quanjing).

Tools and Materials

Paper cutting requires scissors and paper. But you must choose tools that fit you to get the desired result.

Scissors. There is a large variety of scissors on the market. To find a pair that is right for you, follow these five principles.

Point. To use regular scissors for paper cutting, you can sharpen the point as necessary to make it more acute and smooth. The scissors' point determines whether snip and edges are sleek and smooth.

Cutting blade. A sharp blade is a vital element. If the blade is dull, it can affect the speed of the cut. The quality of the cut edges will also be reduced, creating uneven, rough lines that are not as attractive.

Blade back. Keep the back of the blade clean and smooth to prevent snags or scratches on the paper surface.

Score. When buying scissors, confirm the tightness and the responsiveness of the score. If the score is too tight, you will have problems opening and closing the blade with too much resistance. It could also destroy the paper.

Handle. Everyone's hand is different. Choose a handle that fits your hand. If the handle is too small, it will be difficult to put leverage into the cut. If the handle is too large, the scissors will be unwieldy. In addition, a wrong handle size can cause scissors to slip out of your hands, causing paper rips and even injury to your own hands.

Children should use children's scissors to avoid injury. Also, they should be supervised by an adult when cutting paper.

Paper. Paper is the basic material for paper cutting. Choosing the right paper not only makes every part of

paper cutting more convenient; it can also highlight the theme of the artwork.

Waxed paper. This type of paper has a shiny surface and tends to be thin, which makes for easy folding. It is also easier for paper cutting with hollowed out patterns. Some waxed paper come in a choice of print; you can choose according to the theme of the art piece. Chinese people generally prefer to use red waxed paper for paper cutting projects. It brings a festive mood to holidays and celebrations, and is the most traditional paper used in paper cutting.

Color paper. This type of paper comes in a variety of colors. Compared to waxed paper, color paper is more brittle, but is also more crisp, which makes it suitable for works that need to hold their shape. In the process of cutting, avoid creating coarse or rough edges.

Magazine paper. Magazine paper comes in a variety of thickness. Choose the thickness based on the artwork and desired outcome. Another advantage of magazine paper is the randomness of print and texts on the paper, which can create delightful unexpected results. Also, you can recycle while creating art.

Cardstock. Cardstock is thick, which can make cutting difficult as well as create coarse edges. But cardstock is the ideal choice for making greeting cards. The final product can hold its shape very well.

Accessories

By adding accessories, paper cutting projects can become lively and versatile ornaments.

Rope. Turn paper cutting projects into door or window curtains. Choose hemp or linen rope that is thick and which will not break easily. Secure paper cutting projects to the rope with paper clips or glue. You can put as many paper patterns on the rope as you like.

Thread. Use thread to string together paper cuttings to create wind chimes. Use thin thread to allow movement.

Picture frames. Frames are made from different materials. Choose according to the theme of the artwork as well as the gift recipient and the usage. For example, for gifts to elders, choose a dark color in a sturdy, elegant material. For children, choose a bright color and a lighter material.

Color ribbons. Choose a color, length, and width that match the paper cutting and use it for gift-wrapping. You may also choose a more rustic ribbon such as hemp for a simpler style.

White glue. An environmentally friendly product that can be used to paste together paper cutting pieces or to adhere works to various objects and surfaces.

Color beads and sequins. Beads and sequins can be strung onto threads to decorate wind chimes or banners. They can also be glued onto pictures or patterns to add color and stereoscopic feeling to flat paper cutting projects.

Color pencils. Add creative touches to paper cuttings. For example, write a blessing or a greeting, add a poem, draw a simple sketch, or paint a background. You may also create your personal signature and add to each paper cutting as a logo.

Tools, materials and accessories for paper cutting.

How to Use This Book

This book highlights common holidays and celebrations from everyday life so the reader can conveniently choose at leisure. In just three simple steps, you can create a nice paper cutting project. Step 1: understand the inner meaning of the pattern, and choose an appropriate project that you like. Step 2: cut along the dotted lines on the project. Step 3: use the paper cutting directly, or add decorative accessories to embellish the final work.

Follow these three points to maximize the use of this book:

1. This book lists over 100 design patterns, almost all of which symbolize auspicious fortunes, happiness, beauty and harmony; they all represent wishes for a good life. Although the patterns belong to different categories, they can all be mixed and matched. For example, the Valentine's Day silhouette can be used for a wedding anniversary greeting card.

2. Each page lists the complete design patterns. You can copy or print them in a proportionate size suitable for your desired projects. For example, you can shrink a pattern for a greeting card, or you can enlarge another pattern for a large lampshade.

3. You can choose a desired pattern, and scan or trace the pattern onto a material of your choice. When necessary, use an X-Acto knife to engrave the pattern.

Stir your imagination and design skill, and you will maximize the use of this book and bring color and creativity to your everyday life.

Rose-colored lotus flowers and deep green leaves reflect brightly against each other to create a beautiful scene.

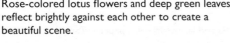

CHAPTER ONE
BIRTHDAY

Birthday celebrations are a tradition enjoyed all over the world. Whether it is birthday parties for children and youth, or banquets for the elderly; with a little thought and imagination—for example, in decorating the party venue, or in a special gift-wrap—you can fascinate the birthday boy or girl, young and old. This chapter features birthday blessings in two sections: the twelve horoscopes and longevity blessings.

The twelve horoscopes represent the different birth months. They are: Aries, Taurus, Gemini, Cancer, Leo, Virgo, Libra, Scorpio, Sagittarius, Capricorn, Aquarius, and Pisces. What will happen when we combine Western horoscope patterns with the Eastern art of paper cutting?

Birthday banquets for the elderly are a traditional custom in China, which can be traced back to the Spring and Autumn Period (771–476 B.C.), when society's upper class practiced customs related to longevity blessings. Generally, birthday banquets are initiated by the junior generations, who invite close family and friends to celebrate together. During the banquet, the younger generations will perform a longevity blessing ceremony, as well as eat birthday noodles together. Friends and family usually bring peaches, poem couplets, and paintings, etc. as gifts. The themes of couplets and paintings usually include homophones, combined with common animals and plants, as expressions of good wishes.

This is a birthday blessing pattern. Two paradise flycatchers fly gently as if they are about to land on two white magnolia flowers. The paradise flycatcher is an auspicious bird, with beautiful colorful feathers, and an elongated tail that symbolizes longevity. The white magnolia, which represents virtue and purity, can also point to the recipient's noble character. This work performs double duty as both a blessing and praise.

For birthday parties for the elderly, place table lamps adorned with paper cuttings of the "five blessings for longevity" design in the party rooms. A purple design on frosted glass appears sophisticated and luxurious against the backdrop of yellow light, depicting the high respectable status of the elderly.

The phoenix is another auspicious creature in Chinese culture, having experienced nirvana and rebirth. This pattern joins the Chinese character for longevity (*shou*, 寿) and phoenix with wings in full bloom, combining the flexibility of paper cutting with the strict structure of Chinese characters. How unique!

Both this two designs are named "five blessings for longevity," widely spread in folk culture. In the center of each design is the circular character for longevity in seal script, surrounded by five bats. Because the word for bat (*fu*, 蝠) is a homophone of the word for blessing (*fu*, 福), the five bats represent the five blessings of longevity, wealth, peace, virtue, and a life that ends well. Together, the design as a whole is a blessing of longevity and a good life.

Aries (March 21–April 19)

The symbol for Aries is a ram. Because it begins on the first day of spring, it represents a new beginning, like the earth has been reborn, fresh and thriving.

Taurus (April 20–May 20)

Taurus represents "creation"; at the same time, it symbolizes beauty and artistry. Individuals under the Taurus sign count persistence as their greatest feature.

Gemini (May 21–June 21)
Gemini is represented by the inseparable twin stars, Castor and Pollux. It is often viewed as the symbol of a dual character. Gemini is also a symbol of wisdom.

Cancer (June 22–July 22)
Cancer is a constellation full of kindness and warmth. Its symbol is a crab carrying a hard shell, which indicates strength of character.

Leo (July 23–August 22)
Leo is represented by the king of beasts. Leos are very attractive. They continually try and express themselves, as a way to explore their own potential and abilities.

Virgo (August 23–September 22)
Virgo is the embodiment of the pursuit for perfection. This pattern for Virgo is a young woman holding a bundle of grain. It symbolizes the hard work of harvesting wisdom.

Libra (September 23–October 23)

Libra's symbol is a scale, which represents fairness, justice, and balance. Libras are courteous, and are constantly seeking balance.

Scorpio (October 24–November 22)

Scorpio's symbol is a scorpion with a curled tail. It has always been considered a mysterious sign. Its character as both good and evil makes Scorpio the topic of many conversations.

Sagittarius (November 23–December 21)
The symbol for Sagittarius is a centaur: the top half is a human figure holding a bow and arrow, and the bottom half is that of a horse. The human half represents knowledge and wisdom, while the horse represents freedom.

Capricorn (December 22–January 19)
Capricorn is represented by a goat. The goat is an animal that exhibits tenacity and hard work. This is a constellation with earnestness and extraordinary willpower.

Aquarius (January 20–February 18)
Aquarius is represented by a jug pouring water. The water pours out of the jug and is transformed by the flow of air in its environment. It is highly aesthetic, specific yet abstract at the same time. Aquarius represents innovation.

Pisces (February 19–March 20)
Pisces is two fish, intertwined. While they are two independent entities, they are inseparable, reflecting the intrinsic complexity of Pisces.

The Chinese language is a highly profound form of art. With some changes, even a common everyday character can be transformed into a brilliant work of art.

In the design on top, the plum blossom is put together with the word for longevity (*shou*, 寿). The flower blooms during the bitingly cold winter when other flowers wither. It is praiseworthy for its virtues of strength, righteousness, and perseverance in the face of struggle. This design is to wish the elderly person health and longevity while praising his character.

The bottom left design is a circular character for longevity. The bottom right design is the character in its traditional form.

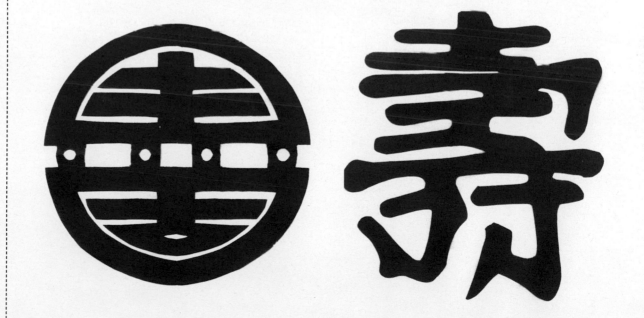

The crane, with its elegant posture, is an immortal bird, a symbol of Taoism. The deer is an auspicious animal; in legends the deer can live for two thousand years. Both creatures are symbols of longevity in Chinese traditional culture. The crane flies freely in the air; while the deer watches in a refined pose. This is called "crane and deer in spring," because spring signifies a remarkable, vibrant life.

In Chinese Taoism culture, the crane is the mount for the immortal, a symbol of longevity. The pine tree stands strong for many years and continues to reach into the clouds. The crane and pine come together to represent a long life with good fortune.

CHAPTER TWO
CELEBRATION FOR THE NEW BORN

The Chinese use a Full Moon Banquet or One-Month-Old Feast to celebrate the arrival of a new baby. The name of the feast—Full Moon Banquet—refers to a full month's time since the birth of the baby. On this day, the parents of the child invite friends and family together to wish blessings upon the child.

The baby is the real star of the feast; everyone wishes the baby to grow up healthy and well. Friends and family bring useful gifts such as hats, baby clothes, and bracelets. Objects with auspicious meanings such as vases and *ruyi* (an ornament used as a symbol of luck) are usually hung on the bracelets. They wish upon the baby a life of smooth sailing and good fortune.

There are many customs associated with the Full Moon Banquet, such as eating noodles, eating peanuts, and party gifts of happiness eggs. Happiness eggs are hard-boiled eggs dyed red. When friends and family come for the banquet, the baby's parents happily give happiness eggs as a thank-you gift. Sometimes they even add candy or chocolates. The gift bag or box is covered with a variety of decorative,

good luck patterns to mean a sweet, beautiful life for the baby.

Whether it is the gift bag from the baby's parents, or the guest's gift box for the baby, use paper cuttings as a complement to the packaging to give more meaning to the gift.

The Chinese zodiac sign under which the baby is born is also an important topic. The Chinese zodiac culture has a long history; twelve animals represent twelve years, and twelve years form a cycle. The twelve animals, in order, are: rat, ox, tiger, rabbit, dragon, snake, horse, sheep, monkey, rooster, dog, and pig. The dragon is the emblem of China; the rest are animals that live in nature. It is popular and convenient to remember birth years by the zodiac sign. And because some animals have meaningful folklores associated with them, it makes this animal calendar notation much more interesting.

This is a longevity lock. It is placed on the baby's neck as a decorative pendant, which can also ward off evil spirits. The patterns around the lock represent good luck, while the text in the center means to live long and never grow old.

Green apple cut-outs complement an orange wine tote. The first character of "apple" (*ping*, 苹) is a homophone of the first character of "peace" (*ping*, 平); therefore it is very appropriate to use apples as a blessing of a life full of peace.

Rat

The rat is the first of the 12 zodiac signs. It represents acumen and wealth. People born in the year of the rat are cheerful, motivated, and independent.

Ox

The ox is hardworking and steadfast; in agricultural society, the ox is a great helper to people. Therefore, the ox is an important theme in paper cutting patterns. This paper cutting ox has a large peony on its body, which highlights Chinese paper cutting's artistic characteristic of being exaggerated.

Tiger

Chinese traditional culture is accustomed to using the image of the fierce tiger to ward off evil spirits. The tiger in this paper cutting pattern has the "king" character (*wang*, 王) clearly visible on its head. While it does not live up to its reputation as the mighty "King of the Beasts," its charmingly naïve appearance reveals a subtle cuteness.

Rabbit

The rabbit likes to run; this clever, cute creature is an auspicious animal. The rabbit in this pattern has just taken a leap towards its favorite carrot.

Dragon

The dragon is the emblem of the Chinese nation. The dragon combines different parts of nine animals into one; they include the shrimp's eyes, the deer's antlers, the cow's mouth, the dog's nose, the catfish's whiskers, the lion's mane, the snake's tail, fish scales, and the eagle talons. The pattern of a dragon playing with a pearl means smooth sailing and wishes coming true.

Snake

In Chinese mythology, Nüwa, the Goddess creator of mankind, is half woman and half snake. This shows the nobility and power associated with the snake. The snake in this paper cutting pattern has many different shapes on its skin. Its coiled body glides across the grass with agility.

Horse

The horse has been the main driving force behind agricultural production, transportation, and military activities since ancient times. Thus, many Chinese proverbs and idioms use the horse to represent leadership and success. In this paper cutting pattern, a horse steps on clouds, symbolizing soaring ambitions and determination.

Sheep

Sheep have a gentle, kind, and pure nature. In Chinese characters, "sheep" (*yang*, 羊) matches "auspicious" (*xiang*, 祥), so sheep symbolize good luck and happiness. In this paper cutting design, the curl pattern on the body represents fluffy fur. The hoofs stride over fortune clouds, which gives an even deeper "lucky" meaning.

Monkey

Monkeys are smart and cute, and are commonly seen in Chinese literature. For example, in one of the four great Chinese classical novels, *Journey to the West*, Sun Wukong, also known as the Monkey King, is an omnipotent hero from the heavens. Also, because the character for "monkey" (*hou*, 猴) matches "nobleman" (*hou*, 侯), monkeys have also come to represent the beautiful meaning of rising up in the world.

Rooster

The rooster is the most common livestock. The Chinese word for "rooster" (*ji*, 鸡) is a homophone of the word for "good luck" (*ji*, 吉), so roosters have symbolized good luck for ages.

Tiger

Chinese traditional culture is accustomed to using the image of the fierce tiger to ward off evil spirits. The tiger in this paper cutting pattern has the "king" character (*wang*, 王) clearly visible on its head. While it does not live up to its reputation as the mighty "King of the Beasts," its charmingly naïve appearance reveals a subtle cuteness.

Rabbit

The rabbit likes to run; this clever, cute creature is an auspicious animal. The rabbit in this pattern has just taken a leap towards its favorite carrot.

Dragon

The dragon is the emblem of the Chinese nation. The dragon combines different parts of nine animals into one; they include the shrimp's eyes, the deer's antlers, the cow's mouth, the dog's nose, the catfish's whiskers, the lion's mane, the snake's tail, fish scales, and the eagle talons. The pattern of a dragon playing with a pearl means smooth sailing and wishes coming true.

Snake

In Chinese mythology, Nüwa, the Goddess creator of mankind, is half woman and half snake. This shows the nobility and power associated with the snake. The snake in this paper cutting pattern has many different shapes on its skin. Its coiled body glides across the grass with agility.

Horse

The horse has been the main driving force behind agricultural production, transportation, and military activities since ancient times. Thus, many Chinese proverbs and idioms use the horse to represent leadership and success. In this paper cutting pattern, a horse steps on clouds, symbolizing soaring ambitions and determination.

Sheep

Sheep have a gentle, kind, and pure nature. In Chinese characters, "sheep" (*yang*, 羊) matches "auspicious" (*xiang*, 祥), so sheep symbolize good luck and happiness. In this paper cutting design, the curl pattern on the body represents fluffy fur. The hoofs stride over fortune clouds, which gives an even deeper "lucky" meaning.

Dog

The dog is man's closest animal companion. In this paper cutting work, the jagged edge along the body of the dog gives the illusion of soft fur. Add a butterfly above, this cute dog comes alive on paper.

Pig

The pig has a rounded body. It is gentle, well-behaved, and very cute. People believe pigs bring fortune and good luck.

The carp is a lucky symbol, and is one of the most broadly used patterns in Chinese traditional decorations. The word for "fish" (*yu*, 鱼) sounds the same as "extra" (*yu*, 余), and thus the fish represents abundance and perfection. Use the fish as a theme to make a heartfelt wish for the baby to have a promising future and a life of fortune. In this paper cutting pattern, the lively fish jumps, highlighting the baby's liveliness. The three text characters above (from right to left) indicate a long life for the child.

In China, another name for the peanut is "long life fruit." The plump peanut is like the chubby body of a baby, making it even more adorable.

Monkey

Monkeys are smart and cute, and are commonly seen in Chinese literature. For example, in one of the four great Chinese classical novels, *Journey to the West*, Sun Wukong, also known as the Monkey King, is an omnipotent hero from the heavens. Also, because the character for "monkey" (*hou*, 猴) matches "nobleman" (*hou*, 侯), monkeys have also come to represent the beautiful meaning of rising up in the world.

Rooster

The rooster is the most common livestock. The Chinese word for "rooster" (*ji*, 鸡) is a homophone of the word for "good luck" (*ji*, 吉), so roosters have symbolized good luck for ages.

CHAPTER THREE
WEDDINGS AND ANNIVERSARIES

The wedding day and anniversaries are among the most romantic moments in a person's life. On wedding day, a couple takes each other's hand to enter a new life together. As the old Chinese poem goes, "I take your hand and grow old with you." On their wedding anniversary day, husband and wife who have weathered the storms of life together take each other's hand again to bear witness to the past and to look towards the future together.

In China, red is the theme color of weddings, unlike the white used in the western. However, modern lifestyle pursues a mixture of east and west, resulting in unintended trends. The use of paper cutting in weddings has also been enriched. For example, paper cuttings are used in decorative drapery, name cards for dinner guests, wedding invitations, even on dinner menus. They add a festive touch to the occasion. Typical patterns include the Chinese character for "happiness," a pair of mandarin ducks that symbolize yin and yang, a heart, or a pair of swans.

The main stars of a wedding anniversary might be an elderly couple with white hair, or they might be newlyweds still enjoying their sweet time after marriage. The momentous occasion of the anniversary day can deepen their affection. To celebrate this sweet moment, it is essential to have a party unlike any other. The most grand include the silver 25th anniversary, the golden 50th anniversary, and the diamond 60th anniversary. Wedding day paper cutting patterns can also be used for anniversary parties.

Whether attending a wedding for a young new couple, or as a guest at an anniversary party; whether presenting a paper cutting piece as a gift, or using paper cutting to decorate a gift; these are all unique ways to surprise the recipient.

Pomegranates have numerous crystal clear fruits inside, which have come to represent the blessing of many descendants. Use pomegranates to wish the newlyweds a blissful marriage and the blessing of a child.

Add a peony floral design to a wedding invitation, or use a peony paper cutting as a seal for the envelope to add a festive touch.

Peonies represent wealth and richness. Their large shape and thick, overlapping petals symbolize completeness, abundance, and wellness. They bring a festive, auspicious atmosphere to weddings and anniversaries.

Three large melons are connected to a curling vine to mean, "to extend without a break, to breed and nourish." Use this design to bless the couple with a hope of many generations to thrive and prosper.

The magpie is an auspicious bird. To hear the song of a magpie means happiness is coming. The word for plum blossom (*mei*, 梅) sounds like the word for eyebrows (*mei*, 眉); therefore, seeing a magpie on a plum blossom denotes "happiness upon the eyebrows," meaning a happy event is about to bring joy to one's face. Add a double happiness design to the top, and it's happiness upon happiness.

Cherries hang on branches at their peak ripeness and abundance. The eye-catching fruit is deep red like carnelian gemstones; their color reveals a sweet sentiment. The blessing is for the newlywed couple to have a beautiful love and a joyful life together.

The lily symbolizes "hundred of years" of marital bliss or a "hundred" wishes coming true. The first character in the word for lily means "a hundred" and the second character means "together" or "fitting." Because of its elegant shape and its fresh, pure white color, the lily is often indispensible as wedding decorations. Lilies bless the newlyweds with a fulfilling married life.

This is a pair of joy pots. On top of each handle is a pair of magpies, which are symbols of luck. The crane and pine evergreen on the body of the pot symbolize a blessing of long life. Together, the symbols wish upon the newlyweds a life of fulfilling harmony and long lasting love.

This piece utilizes exaggerated distortion to place a pair of mandarin ducks in the center of a lotus flower. Mandarin ducks are traditionally used as symbols of a perfect love, of two soul mates having been brought together. The lotus flower has an elegant shape and an air of excellence; at the same time, it is the emblem of Buddhism, a symbol of purity. The lotus is often together with aquatic animals such as mandarin ducks to symbolize a loving marriage.

Swans are monogamous, and thus is a symbol of loyal love. The lotus flower is elegant. The combination of swan and lotus symbolizes the purity of love and a harmonic marriage.

This design combines a chubby baby with a lotus flower, a lotus root, and a lotus seed pod. It symbolizes the blessing of many generations to fill the house, and a harmonious, joyful life.

The child is the blessing upon the family of two and has close relationships with both the father and the mother.

Children are a family's source of joy and laughter. From two people on a wedding day to four people on a wedding anniversary day means joy and happiness.

This is the silhouette of a white-haired elderly couple, revealing tenderness despite the rough lines. Even though the couple is showing wrinkles, they face each other with eyes full of love and care. Whether it is for parents or grandparents, present them with this silhouette paper cutting to make them smile.

CHAPTER FOUR
GRADUATION AND PROMOTION

In China there is an old saying that illustrates four joyful occasions in life. They are: a nourishing rain after a long drought; an old friend in a foreign place; a candle lit wedding night; and a name on the scholars list. The "name on the scholars list" in today's world would point to two occasions: graduation or job advancement.

Graduation parties are always inspiring. What kind of invitation card can show some originality? Are you tired of boring wall hangings made of crepe paper and lifeless balloons? How can you make the dinner menu stand out from all the others? What kind of gift would be unforgettable for the recipient? What kind of decorations would bring delight to the host? The answers can all be found here.

As for job advancement, whether it is a small promotion or a big step forward, a party or even a small gathering is essential. Whether you wish to thank friends or family for the support and help, or if others want to congratulate you, it can all be opportunities to build and strengthen relationships. As with graduation parties, some thought must be invested into the planning.

Therefore, choose a design and let's start working!

Whether it is a bachelor, masters, or a doctorate cap, it is a result of hard work on the road of scholarship. It is deeply meaningful, whether you are making this for yourself or other students around you.

Place a personal favorite paper cutting inside a frame to make it convenient to enjoy as well as to preserve it. It is also more presentable as a gift. This smooth sailing pattern represents a wish that everything will go well, and is suitable for many occasions.

The bow of the ship points forward; the sail is full, rousing the waves beneath the ship. This image of breaking waves with a strong sail is clear. It symbolizes smooth sailing in scholarship and business along the road of life.

A carp jumps towards the dragon's gate. If it crosses the gate it becomes a dragon. This is a story in Chinese mythology, which says that through hard work, one can have a meteoric rise overnight, and go from an ordinary citizen to a "dragon" (or a standout star) among the people. This illustrates a hope for a steady rise in scholarship, work, and life overall.

The persimmon is a good luck charm symbol in traditional Chinese culture. The word for persimmon (*shi*, 柿) sounds like the word for business or happenings (*shi*, 事); put two persimmons together to mean everything would happen as one wishes.

This flying horse has two fully spread wings and legs striding across the clouds, symbolizing a swift, strong success. Use this to send wishes of fast, smooth, easy success at the start of school or start of a business.

The hard work and diligence of an ox can very often yield good fruits. This ox has a large muscular body, four strong hooves, and horns pointing forward, demonstrating a fierce, continuous power moving forward. Use this to wish that the recipient could also forge ahead courageously and prosper.

Plum blossom money utilizes a string of Chinese copper coins to accompany the plum blossom petals on top; this represents good fortune, longevity, luck, and wealth. And because it sounds like "bad luck gone," placing this design in the office would contribute to smooth business and career advancement.

Bamboo is a symbol commonly seen in traditional Chinese culture. In Chinese, there is an idiom called "bamboo established in the heart," which means, before the bamboo is painted, the full image of the bamboo has already been established in the mind. This represents confidence, that before taking the first step on an endeavor, there is already certainty of success. Thus, bamboo can be used to bless the recipient with success in work or school.

This paper cutting design is composed of three patterns; from top to bottom they are green beans, copper coins, and a katydid. Green beans represent four seasons of peace, health, and joy; the copper coin represents roiling riches; the katydid, with its chirp and its strong leap, symbolizes a fast rising up of the ranks. This composition is a perfect gift for someone being promoted.

This is a toad with only three legs, with a plump body and aiming upward with a coin in the mouth. This pattern is called "a golden toad beckoning money." Use it as a blessing that business would boom, and that riches would be abundant; this will definitely make a good impression.

As the bamboo shoot continues to aim upward and grow, it can one day match the height of the bamboo. Each person's journey is like that of a bamboo shoot— one must continuously rise to the challenge and aim upward in order to achieve the grand blueprint of the heart. This artful piece is a perfect gift for recent graduates entering the workforce of society.

CHAPTER FIVE
HOUSEWARMING

Moving into a new house is a joyous occasion. A housewarming party is an essential part of a new house; it can liven up the mood of a new space while providing an opportunity to reconnect with friends and family. Whether you are the host decorating the house, or the guest bringing gifts, there are many opportunities to show mutual affection. Friends and family usually bring housewarming gifts, such as framed paintings, decorative ornaments, household items, wine, etc. Generally, images of bats represent fortune, peonies represent wealth, peacocks represent grandeur, etc. The host entertains the guests as a show of gratitude.

Chinese people also have the tradition of what's called a "stable house." To make a "stable" house means to protect the stability, peace, and safety of the household. It is intricately intertwined with the Chinese art of feng shui. This process is a very important aspect of moving and housewarming. Most people use specific decorations and furnishings to achieve the goal of stabilizing a house, to ward off evil spirits that might invade a house or the family's relationships. Some examples arc fish tanks, crystals, and animal carvings and ornaments. The themes range from natural objects to mythical beasts, such as dragons, *pixiu*, or unicorns, because in Chinese mythology these creatures have the power to protect a house. There are also some animal symbols, such as the golden jaguar and the elephant, which bring wealth to the house owner.

Nandina is slightly red when young, becoming violet red in autumn. Its Chinese name is a homonym for "blessing from Heaven," implying the elimination of all evil things.

This pattern, on green background with golden embellishments, use the symbols of gold fish and seaweed to say "gold and jade fill the halls." The square composition of the paper cutting echoes beautifully with the simplicity of the round white decorative plate. Whether as a housewarming gift or for decoration, this makes a unique choice.

Gold fish are small and exquisite, with rich vibrant colors; they swim in a pond as if dancing elegantly between water plants and seaweeds. The gold in gold fish represents wealth; the word for fish (*yu*, 鱼) sounds like the word for jade (*yu*, 玉), a symbol of great wealth. Place an aquarium of gold fish in the house to bring in great wealth that fills the home.

The *pixiu* is a ferocious yet auspicious creature from ancient Chinese mythology. It can swallow a thousand things and not spill a single drop; therefore, it represents obtaining riches from all facets of life. It can ward off evil and bring joy; the best of luck come to those who own one. This paper cutting also uses exaggerated images to show a ferocious *pixiu* who is also lovable.

Deer are a very common auspicious animal in traditional Chinese culture. They have four slender legs and a pair of beautiful antlers. Because the word for deer (*lu*, 鹿) sounds like the word for road (*lu*, 路), two deer standing together have come to mean a smooth road ahead. The word for deer also sounds like the word for wealth (*lu*, 禄); therefore, two deer also can mean double wealth and luck. Whether it is smooth road ahead or abundant riches and luck, give the host a pair of deer to bring good luck to the house during housewarming.

The golden jaguar has a strong body that can jump and run extremely well. In this work, the golden jaguar is leaping high into the air with four extended legs, creating a beautiful silhouette in mid-air. Because the pattern on the body of a golden jaguar is very similar to the shape of ancient copper coins, the golden jaguar is often used to represent wealth and riches.

The elephant is a benevolent animal; its warm demeanor is always popular. The elephant in this work bears a large fungus on its back. This is an image for good luck, because the word for elephant is a homophone of the word for auspicious; this particular fungus is also a symbol of wishes coming true, therefore it also means good luck. The two combine seamlessly together to present a blessing of wishes coming true and great luck.

When a peacock spreads its beautiful feathers, it has a graceful posture; the peacock is often paired with flowers such as peonies to represent great fortune and luck. Try using this pattern to accompany flowers or other floral objects as gifts, to present a blessing of a brilliant life like that of a blooming peacock.

The magpie is an auspicious bird. Magpies' coming to the house means good things are about to happen.

Bamboos grow very quickly, and year after year they grow taller and taller. Bamboo in the house means a vibrant, growing family that reaches great new heights year after year.

Two magpies perched on plum blossom branches symbolize unending good luck and double happiness. The plum blossom petals are round and plump, occasionally accompanied by cute tiny buds, which makes this picture particularly lively. As for the two magpies, one is chirping to the sky with its head raised, while the other resonates with its head turned. The entire work moves in perfect symphony, as is the atmosphere of a great housewarming.

CHAPTER SIX
NEW YEAR

The three Chinese characters from left to right mean "Happy New Year."

Chinese New Year is considered the most important holiday of the year. In the west, New Year falls on January 1st, and Chinese people call this the New Year's Day. For the Chinese, the new year starts on Spring Festival, on the first day of the lunar calendar. Spring Festival celebrations on this day are even more grand, and Spring Festival is the most valued holiday for Chinese people all around the world. On this day, no matter how far apart, everyone has to go home for a family reunion.

There are many celebrations and activities associated with Spring Festival. Some customs even have thousands of years of history. Out with the old, in with the new, is the motto. Every single household must have a thorough cleaning before the arrival of the new year as a symbol of renewal; the intent is to remove bad luck and usher in new beginnings. The new year is a huge opportunity to use paper cuttings.

First, there are window decorations. Place bright red floral paper cuts on windows to heighten the festive mood; they play triple purpose of decoration, beauty, and practicality. At night, as light filters through the window, beautiful silhouettes and shadows are the result. These days, there are even paper cutting stickers that can be placed on doors or curtains to really bring a blast of red color throughout the home.

Another way is to place colorful paper cuttings on top of ceramic plates or porcelain bowls full of fruits and candies. This bodes well for a sweet new year and great new heights.

Friends and families also practice the tradition of visiting each other. Every one exchanges gifts and greeting cards, and wishes upon each other a year of smooth sailing and family harmony. Paper cuttings can bring a layer of novelty to any gift or greeting card.

Popular designs for new year include the God of Wealth, carp fish to represent abundance, small pigs that represent wealth, and a treasure bowl to represent a roiling arrival of cash, etc.

Paper cuts with floral patterns in circular forms are an essential element of Chinese New Year. The peonies intertwined inside the circle present a posture of wonderful grace and richness. The elegant thin lines of the paper cutting echo the slender branches on the right for an extremely classy portrait.

On Chinese New Year's Eve, Chinese people set off firecrackers to liven up the atmosphere of the festivities.

A treasure bowl filled with gold bullions and jewels has always been a symbol of the pursuit of wealth. During the start of a new year, use a treasure bowl to bless the household with abundant riches.

On every New Year's Day or Spring Festival, hanging red lanterns is an indispensible tradition. The red color of the lantern represents the thriving business of the coming year, and the roundness of the lantern shape symbolizes the wholeness of family unity.

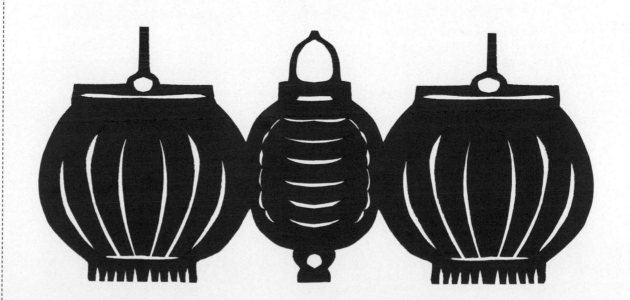

These three flowers are peony, crabapple, and magnolia (from top to bottom). The first word of magnolia means jade (*yu*, 玉); and the second word of crabapple sounds similar to hall (*tang*, 堂). These two words together sound like *yutang*, which means rich and elite family. The peony, with its rich elegant posture, represents wealth. Therefore, these three flowers together represent a blessing for prosperity and wealth.

This design has a vase embellished with peonies. The word for vase (*ping*, 瓶) is a homophone of the word for peace (*ping*, 平). Peonies are a symbol of beauty and riches. Together, they bode well for a new year of tranquility and riches.

The word for fish (*yu*, 鱼) sounds like the word for extra (*yu*, 余); therefore, fish is used to hope for extra abundance and riches in the new year.

CHAPTER SEVEN
VALENTINE'S DAY

Valentine's Day falls on February 14th of every year. This is a holiday about love and romance; a day embellished with flowers, chocolates, and Valentine's Day cards. Men and women who love and admire each other exchange gifts to show affection on this day. In China, in addition to Valentine's Day on February 14th, couples also celebrate the seventh day of the seventh month on the lunar calendar. This day is called Qixi Festival (also called the Double Seventh Festival), and there is a beautiful love story behind the tradition.

A long time ago, the legend says, an orphan named Niulang ("the cowherd") fell in love with a fairy named Zhinü ("the weaver girl"). They made an eternal commitment, and gave birth to two beautiful children, a boy and a girl. However, the news of the weaver girl's marriage to a mere mortal reached the heavenly courts, which brought the weaver girl back to the heavens and decreed the couple could only be allowed to meet once a year, on the 7th day of the 7th month of the year. Numerous flocks of magpies would fly together to form a bridge, whereupon the weaver girl could reunite with her beloved Niulang and their two children. Later, on the 7th day of the 7th month, young women would look for Niulang and Zhinü in the stars on the two opposite sides of the Milky Way. Today, Qixi Festival is not only a festival for couples, but also a festival for young women.

Of course, whether it is the western Valentine's Day or the Chinese Qixi Festival, put a little thought into decorating a gift or a card with paper cuttings to make each other feel deeply loved.

Patterns commonly associated with couples include a pair of swallows flying side-by-side, a pair of mandarin ducks, and silhouettes of a dancing couple, etc. Why not propose on Valentine's Day, and present a ring box personally decorated with a decoupage?

Roses are necessities on Valentine's Day.

A gift inside a royal blue heart-shaped box is a top choice for a couple. Place a pink-colored paper cutting on the box to show your extra touch of thoughtfulness.

Before every beautiful
wedding, there is a romantic
proposal. The man gets down
on one knee to present a
rose to a woman. A rose
represents a beautiful love.
The woman accepts and two
young hearts are thus forever
intertwined.

The plum blossom represents loyalty and elegance. The male and female swallows flying together is a symbol of love. This pair of swallows flies towards the plum blossom together, like a young couple entering a beautiful new life alongside each other.

This is a heart-shaped garland, composed by eight graceful paradise flycatchers carrying plum blossoms which are fresh and elegant.

Having an even number of birds denotes "completeness"; the word for plum blossom sounds like "eyebrows," indicating respectfulness and intimacy between a couple in Chinese idiom. Together, they mean "completeness and togetherness," used as a blessing for a loving couple.

A pair of mandarin ducks facing each other is a symbol of eternal love. Lotus means sacredness. This design embodies two people loving and caring for each other.

Roses are love and beauty in one. They play an essential role on Valentine's Day. Their colors are rich and bright, and their flower shapes are delicate and pretty. A purple rose represents a guardian of love.

The unwavering love of the cowherd and the weaver girl touched generations. For ages since, the story has come to describe affectionate lovers.

At a party, the couple in love dance happily. For them being in love can be merry like a melodious song.

CHAPTER EIGHT
MOTHER'S DAY

Mother's Day falls on the second Sunday in the month of May. In ancient times, to commemorate Hera, the queen of the Gods, the Greek would hold a grand celebration. Although this is a tribute to a goddess, it nonetheless reflects a reverence for motherhood. During the mid-17th century, this practice spread to England. Today, young people who live far away from home would return home and give a small gift to their mother as a token of love.

The modern Mother's Day was initiated by Anna Jarvis (1864–1948), who instituted the second Sunday of May as Mother's Day. Since then, many countries around the world celebrate this holiday.

Filial piety is one of the most important moral virtues in Chinese culture. China has a widely circulated story named "Mencius' Mother Moves Three Times." During the Warring States Period, the mother of the great thinker Mencius moved their home three times just so Mencius could focus on studying and progress up the scholarly ranks. This shows the hard work and effort put into raising a successful child; she is deemed the model example of motherhood in Chinese culture. Although Mother's Day has not been instituted in China, integration with world culture means that many people in China celebrate Mother's Day on the second Sunday of May. On this day, children invite their mothers to dinner to celebrate, or they would prepare cake and other gifts. A bouquet of carnations is a must. These are all ways to express respect and love for their mother.

A mother's sacrifice to her children and family are incalculable. A DIY Mother's Day gift may better express your gratitude. So let's get started!

Tulips have long, straight stalks; the flowers are pot-shaped, and they come in a variety of rich colors. Each species has its own unique name, such as "peerless beauty" and "black queen of night," just like every mother has her own character: gentle, strong, and resolute. Give tulips to mom to wish her a blessing of eternal youth.

Decorate mom's everyday items such as lamp with your handmade paper cuttings, and let mom feel your love, both at work and at home.

In ancient Chinese legend, the phoenix is the queen of birds. It is an auspicious symbol of good fortune, status, and wealth. Give mom a present with a decoration of a phoenix pattern to wish her longevity and refined beauty.

A little lamb kneels as it feeds on its mother's milk as a show of gratitude for her nourishment. This matches an ancient Chinese saying: "In a hundred virtues, filial piety comes first."

The mother panda quietly carries a baby panda under the bamboo forest. It reminds us of being in our mother's arms The love between a mother and a child is very evident.

Carnations are women's sacred flower. They represent beauty and elegance. They come in many colors, have a fresh fragrance, and embody love, beauty, and respect. On Mother's Day, give a carnation to your mother as a way to say, "Mom, I love you."

Orchids stand tall, come in elegant colors, and have a full-bodied fragrance that is not overpowering. Use orchids to express gratitude and admiration of mom's wisdom and gentleness.

Since birth, every child is cradled in the mother's arms and fed with sweet milk. A mother gives life and also gives the ingredients for growth. This is the essence of a mother's greatness.

A mother uses her delicate arms to raise up her own beloved child as if holding up her own sun, using her strength to fight for more for the child, so the child would have an even better life. On Mother's Day, use this image to thank mother and hope it will bring a smile to her face.

A mother holds her daughter's small hand as she looks back with love. A daughter looks up at her mother, wondering if she will grow up with as much grace and beauty.

CHAPTER NINE
FATHER'S DAY

Every year, the third Sunday in June is Father's Day. This is a special day to give thanks to your father.

Father's Day and Mother's Day have the same purpose and meaning. Behind the image of a hardworking mother, there is always a father with a brawny chest; together they carry a family. A father's love has fortitude and dignity, yet is also close and kind. The world's first Father's Day was born in 1910 in the United States, advocated by Mrs. Dodd in Washington state. After Mrs. Dodd's mother died, her father took up the responsibility of raising and educating six children. After Mrs. Dodd's advocacy, the day finally became a permanent memorial day, and eventually spread throughout the world.

On this day, people like to give gifts of cards, ties, and razors—all very practical, everyday items. Add a personal touch with DIY decorative paper cuttings on the gift box, greeting card, mug, or desk lamp to make these common gifts extra special. As people say, it is the thought that matters more than the gift. Use a heart of gratitude to make something special, and it will bring extra joy to your father.

Green tea has an alluring aroma and a simple elegant taste. It is also beneficial. On Father's Day, prepare a cup of green tea for father, and sit down for a heart-to-heart talk. Give him a blessing of youth and strength, like the crane and the pine on the teapot.

Present father with a gift of tea, and decorate the tin with a pine tree paper cutting. Find some time to have tea and chat with dad, and wish him eternal youth like the evergreen pine.

A father is like a tall tree, protecting the family from the windy storms. Even though a father's love may not be as explicit as a mother's love, it is nonetheless very deep and sturdy, just like a tall tree standing solid as a rock on the earth.

Each person has his or her own unique image of a father that has nothing to do with the father's appearance, because his silhouette, smile, and mannerisms have long been impressed upon the child's heart. The father in this work wears glasses perched on his nose and a hat on his head; his expression is solemn, as if deep in thought.

Owls are the physical incarnation of wisdom. In this design, the two owls' large round eyes are charming. The owl father's sturdy, strong wing holds up the little owl, just like a father who picked up his child and placed him on his shoulder.

When a father penguin hatches an egg, he uses his own back to block the cold wind and snow, protecting the egg. Give this adorable picture to dad as a show of gratitude for his providing everything for our upbringing.

The father elephant is the family's defender. But he also accompanies his baby elephant in playful baths. It is like a father who worked hard all day, but still comes home to happily play with his children.